Write it!

Write it!
How to write your book in 30 hours or less

Adam Jackson

Copyright © 2012 Adam Jackson

Contents

	page
Introduction	4
1 - Why write a book?	7
2 - Creating time to write	16
3 - Creating the working office	25
4 - Motivation and momentum	38
5 - Six habits of every successful writer	41
6 - Generating ideas (hour 1)	45
7 - Research part one (hour 2)	52
8 - Creating an outline (hours 3-4)	54
9 - Writing (hours 5-13)	65
10 - Research part two (hour 14)	70
11 - Editing (hours 15-25)	71
12 - Completion (hours 26-30)	76

Introduction

The Internet has revolutionised the way writers can choose to approach both their writing and how they make their work available to readers. More importantly readers can now choose the books they want to read rather than the books publishers decide should be read.

No longer do you have to agree a deal with a publisher and then wait months before your book appears in selected bookstores; you can choose what you write, decide how and when you make your book available and start selling in a timeframe that suits you and your readers.

Of course you still have to write the best book you can, but how many times have you read something and said, "I could have done better." You still have to promote your work in order to make sales, but, if you prefer, this can all be done online.

Using the method detailed in this book you will be able to plan, write and edit a 20,000 word book in just 30 hours. Remember this is not just a first draft but a book that will generate you income.

That's one hour a day for one month. A month not fast enough for you? Take a week off work and complete your book in a week. Use the weekend to publish and market your book and you could be making sales in just seven days.

You will learn ways to generate ideas every time you need one, you can even quickly come up with a whole series!

Learn how to focus your research so you only spend time on what you need to know.

Using a keyboard and word-processor you will complete your first draft in just nine hours, that's typing at 40 words per minute which is an achievable speed even if you are not a touch typist. Want to write faster – you will learn the fastest way ever to get your words down, you could increase your output fourfold.

Find free tools that will help you succeed as a writer and finally, add those finishing touches so you are recognised as a professional writer.

The first chapters of this book cover some essentials to removing barriers to writing including creating the time, setting up an office and staying motivated. However if you want to get started right away jump straight to chapter 6 and start your book today, you can always come back to the earlier chapters.

This is the start of your journey to writing and finishing your book.

1 - Why write a book?

Many people dream of writing a book and, more often, writing for a living. Most never achieve that dream. Why? Because they never actually complete their book, some don't even start. You are different, you have taken the first step to realising that dream. Follow the steps in this book and you will be looking at your completed and ready to publish book in just thirty hours.

If you are looking to supplement your current income or develop a full-time writing career that provides you with a generous income, enables you to work when and where you choose and also have a great life balance then writing, publishing and selling your book is for you.

You could set up your office in a location of your choice - work from home, on the beach, in the park or in a café. In fact, because you can do much of the work away from the computer, you set the rules, you set your schedule, and you are in control.

Using the method described in Write it! you will complete a 20,000 word book, ready to publish, in 30 hours. That includes research, writing, editing and adding those finishing touches. Writing for an hour a day and complete your book in a month; 3 hours a day you could be looking at your completed manuscript in just 10 days time; take a week off work and complete in a week.

Three reasons to write a book

Money. Lifestyle. Fame. 95% of people give at least one of these reasons when asked why they want to write a book. Nearly everyone will answer money or lifestyle; fame is more personal; if you don't want it, that's fine, just use pen names to keep your true identity hidden until you are ready to reveal all. Of course there are other reasons people want to write a book including the desire to get their story told; this is both valid and a great motivator. Take a look at these three reasons and decide which is more important to you.

Money – how much to you want to earn this year? Probably a bit more than you are earning right now. What if you could triple your current income? Would you sit down and start writing or would you just keep procrastinating. The reality is you decide how much you want to earn and you then start writing, publishing and selling your books. What could be more satisfying than waking in the morning, logging into your sales

account and see that you have made money whilst sleeping? It's a simple equation:
application = income.

Lifestyle – do you really want to be stuck in that traffic jam, taking that long train journey, having holidays when it is convenient with your colleagues, walking the dog in the dark, or would you rather set your own working hours, be able to go to the gym when it is quieter, or take a holiday tomorrow just because the sun is shining? You still have to put the hours in and produce the goods but you choose when and where.

As your income increases you will be able to make some of those lifestyle changes that inspired you to start writing in the first place. You could work from home, work flexible hours, or plan your next book whilst you spend the weekend at the beach or have a barbecue with friends. You decide how many hours you put in and which activities you are going to work on, by doing so you decide your own income. Start generating an income from your first book and you can start living your life your way.

Follow this method and your lifestyle will start to change as soon as you publish your first book.

Start on your second book whilst marketing your first and you will have a ready-made market just waiting for more by the same author.

Fame – not everyone wants fame, but make no mistake whatever name you put on the cover of your book will become famous and your fans will want more books and more interaction. They will want to get to know you and feel like a "personal" friend so you will need to interact with them using social media and blogs to share the life of the author with your fans.

Think very carefully about this, unless you are absolutely sure you personally want this fame then use a pen name, or multiple pen names, you can always link these to the real you at a later date. Of course there are benefits to using your real name – earn money as a speaker, coach others in your area of expertise, support charities by opening events – to name just a few.

Remember: this is your game and your rules.

Why do you want to write?
Before you start it is important you commit to finishing your book; to do this you need to identify your personal dreams and goals.

Do you want to supplement your current income or build a full-time career as a writer? Do you want to work part-time and spend more time with your family or on your hobbies? How much do you want to earn? Remember: application = income.

What would a typical ideal working day look like for you? Would you take a leisurely breakfast and walk the dog before working, or would you get up early and do two hours work before breakfast? What else do you want to do in your day? Go to the gym? Have lunch with friends? You can write your own schedule.

What are your dreams?

So you think you know why you want to write but to keep you focussed and motivated it is important to know why you REALLY want to write a book, what your own personal dreams truly are. Write a list right now of all the things you would buy, change or do if you had the money and time. Don't restrict yourself, you don't have to share this with anyone so no matter how self-centred it may seem write it down. What do you want the money for, do you want to give up your current job, more holidays, a Porsche, a house in the country, more time for your hobbies, more time with family and friends. Try and turn some of these vague dreams into something more specific; is a coastal retreat on your list, if so write down where, how big, any features it should have.

In chapter 4 there is a simple task that you can do that will help you stay focussed on your dreams. You can then refer to it when you just feel too tired to write or feel that other tasks should take priority.

Turning dreams into goals
You now know what your writing will give you but first you have to write that book. You need to set yourself targets, have goals that will move you towards that dream lifestyle. Here is your first target. Write a good book in 30 hours. Follow this method and you will achieve it. This target may seem far removed from reaching the point where you can give up work or buy that coastal retreat, however achieve this target and you can set a target for sales and generating income. Even at this stage you can see that achieving your dream is possible.

Turning dreams into reality

Sometimes our big dreams can appear to be just out of reach; we can see we are moving towards them as we watch our book sales grow but you don't experience it. Set up a dreams-based reward system so that you can start to experience your dream lifestyle as you achieve your targets. Select your top three dreams and start creating mini experiences; attach these to your targets as rewards. As you achieve each target select your reward from the list.

Dream - Coastal retreat

Target - Complete book

- Reward - Day at your favourite coastal town

Target - Sell 1000 copies

- Reward - Book a weekend away in a beach cottage

Dream - Own a Porsche

Target - Complete book

- Reward - Visit a Porsche showroom

Target - Sell 1000 copies

- Reward - Take a Porsche driving experience

Dream – Work from home
Target - Complete book
- Reward - Take a one day holiday from work – and write all day
Target - Sell 1000 copies
- Reward - Take a week of unpaid leave and write everyday

30 hours from now
By the end of Write it! you will be only 30 hours away from having a publishable book, in fact you don't need to wait until the end of this book, you can complete each hour as soon as you have read through the chapter.

With an hour a day you could write ten books in a year. Do the maths, if you earn only £1 for each book sold, how many books a year do you need to sell to replace your current income. Let's say 30,000. Ten books, sell 3,000 of each, that's just 60 books a week of each title, less than 10 a day. Remember if you write a book people enjoy or benefit from they will come back for more so the 3,000 people who buy your first book will buy every book you write. They will be looking for "more titles by this author."

Within a year you may decide to devote a considerable amount of your working week to writing and marketing your work, or even to become a full-time writer.

2 - Creating time to write

"If I had the time I'd write a book," how many times have you heard yourself say this? If and when are the two biggest barriers to completing your book. If you wait until you have the time you will never start, let alone finish, your book. Why? Because you never find time - you create it.

With work and family commitments, jobs around the house, ferrying the kids back and forth, and a multitude of other tasks that mean you get up in the morning and go to bed at night having filled every moment of the day with must-do stuff, it can sometimes seem impossible to even find ten minutes to do something else let alone find an hour each day.

Now I'm not suggesting you neglect your family or give up the day job just yet but you can still create time within your day. Most people can free up fifteen minute slots here and there if you plan ahead; four of these fifteen minute slots gives you the hour a day you need to start and complete your book. Struggle with 15 minute slots? Start with ten minutes at a time.

You are looking to create the time for actively working on your book, you will also need some thinking time but you already have this. Thinking time is available to you when you are doing something that does not require your absolute full attention such as doing the washing–up, walking the dog, mowing the lawn or drinking coffee.

Time thieves

So where does your time go. Identify this and you can start claiming it back. Everyone has time thieves, they pop in unnoticed and steal the odd minute here and there and before you know it those minutes become hours. Here's a list of common time thieves and how to deal with them.

Telephone calls – friends, family, sales calls – before you know it 15 minutes of your valuable writing time has gone – at 40 words per minute that's 600 words. How many phone calls do you make or take in a week (outside of work), three, four, five?

Solution - turn off your telephone, check for messages and missed calls at specific times. Let people leave messages, many people won't bother which probably indicates it was not that important anyway. Batch all of your calls together, both those you need to return and those you choose to make. If you have a number of calls to make you are less likely to engage with small talk. Need a long chat with a friend? Plan the time at the end of your writing session.

Must watch TV – how many soaps do you watch? Serial dramas? Reality shows? Be honest. The problem with these is that they are on regularly, some are on everyday, and you are probably watching more than one. If you are watching one soap, one weekly drama and one news programme you could easily be spending two or three hours a day in front of the TV without even realising it. Add in an extra soap and a sport and suddenly your weekly tally is approaching twenty five hours a week, that's nearly your book finished!

Solution - you need to find out exactly how much TV you are watching, look back on the past week or keep an accurate diary. Don't just include the programmes you choose to watch or like to watch, include everything even if you are only sat there because it is your partner's favourite programme. Remember every 30 minutes watching TV is 1200 words not written. Once you have your TV diary go through this and decide what you need to keep on the "must watch" list. Also note the reason why. Keeping a programme on the list because it is something you all watch as a family is a perfectly valid reason however you need to create some time for writing. Decide which programmes you are no longer going to watch. When they start, leave the room or turn off the TV and start writing. If you find it difficult missing any of your TV shows then try recording at least one programme a day and use this time to write. When you have finished your book you can sit down and catch-up.

Internet – email, social media, browsing. You turn on your computer to use your valuable writing time effectively and what do you do? Check your emails, and then do the replies. See who's doing what on your social media accounts and maybe update your status, and finally just do that bit of research you absolutely need for your book and then get sidetracked with a really interesting site that could form the basis of your next book. You are now twenty minutes into your half hour writing slot and no words written. 800 words lost.

Solution – turn on your computer, do not open your web browser or email account. If you cannot be that disciplined then turn off your broadband router (and wait for the shouts from the rest of the household). Write first and complete your word count, only then start browsing.

Chores – it's a sunny day so you put the washing on, mow the lawn and maybe wash the car. There will always be something else to do. When you are at home, whether full-time, a day off work or even unwell, there will always be jobs that just have to be done. If you were out at work could you do them? You would either leave them until a later time or do them less often.

Solution – do your writing first. Sounds simple but schedule your writing time, complete your word count, and then attack the chores. If you have planned to write at 10.00am then never, ever just finish what you are doing before writing, stop what you are doing and write.

Interruptions – everyone has these, kids want a lift right now, doorbell rings, and your partner needs to tell you about the difficult customer at work. Somebody wants a piece of your time.

Solution – there will be times when you do have to deal with the interruption, most, however, you can actually postpone the need to act until after you have finished your writing slot. It will not take too many times of telling your children, "yes I'll take you but in half an hour," before they realise that they have to plan ahead and fit with your schedule.

Time you didn't know you had

If you have followed the section above you will have claimed back at least half an hour a day from your TV time. You will also have reduced the amount of time that gets stolen from you when you are actually completing a writing session. Now you may still need to find other writing slots during your day to achieve at least an hour of writing time.

Get up earlier – set your alarm clock half an hour earlier. Don't get up and follow your normal routine. If you really need coffee then make a cup but other than that turn on your computer and start writing. If it does not disturb anyone then you could even use a laptop and write in bed.

Go to bed later – maybe you are not a morning person, in that case use the other end of the day. Finish your before bed routine and then write for half an hour. At the end of your planned writing session stop writing. You might want to go on but you will be tired the next day and find it difficult to write during your next session.

Lunch break – do you get an hour for lunch, take back 15 minutes and write. If it is difficult to write in your workplace then go and sit in the car, on a park bench or in a coffee shop. If you do not have access to a computer then use an App on your mobile phone or, as a last resort, hand write in your notebook. Whatever tools you have, get those words down. 200 words are better than no words.

Walking – do you text whilst you walk? Then you can write whilst you walk. No one will take any notice if you are using your phone. Either use an App to type and save your words or send texts to your email account.

Public transport – do you usually drive to work? Could you take public transport and write on the train or bus. With fuel prices as high as they are this might even be a cost effective option.

Schedule your writing time
You should now be seeing where you can create time for your writing; time to take action. Purchase a diary, the type which has a day to a page, includes weekends and preferably has times indicated down the side.

For the next week divide each page into two by drawing a line from top to bottom. On the left hand side allocate your writing slots; think of these as 15 minute slots though you might group some together to create half an hour or an hour. Try and create at least one slot during your previous TV time, a slot at the beginning and/or end of the day and one slot either whilst travelling to work or during a break from work. It is important at this stage to have these three different slots as this will help you develop the habit of being able to write regularly and also to write whenever a slot unexpectedly presents itself.

You should now have identified at least an hour a day for your writing across the next week. Still on the left hand side, against the first time slot make a note of the task you will complete and, if applicable, your target word count; as you complete each time slot note down the task planned for the next slot.

In the right hand side you are going to write in what you actually do with your time. That means the entire day from getting up through to going to bed. Write down all of the things you do; make coffee, sit and drink coffee, read newspaper, have bath. Detail is important here, if you watched TV – what did you watch? Where you have writing slots note how much writing you actually did. If you didn't write during these slots, note why the replacement activity was more important.

At the end of the week look back at your diary and ask yourself these questions:
 - Did I write during my planned writing sessions?
 - Did I achieve my targets during these sessions?
 - Can I reduce interruption to these sessions?
 - Can I be more productive during my writing sessions?
 - Can I identify additional writing sessions?

Now repeat this activity for the following week. Commit to your writing schedule by recording and reviewing it and you will start to see results fast. You will also see where you are procrastinating and how you can become more productive.

3 - Creating the working office

In order to write productively and get your book finished you need to set up a workspace that will enable you to start writing quickly during your scheduled times. If you have to clear the dining table, locate the laptop, get the extension lead because someone has run down the battery, turn it on, wait, and then start writing, well your writing time is not going to be best used. Do this twice a day and you could easily waste half an hour of your valuable writing time. Over 10 weeks this equates to another book.

Your workspace is important; however this does not mean that you cannot write unless you have a dedicated office that no-one else has access to, though you might like to add this to your dreams list.

Setting up your workspace

Three questions often asked by people looking to start writing are - "Do I need an office? Do I need a computer? Do I need expensive software?" Let's take these one at a time.

Do I need an office?
Creating a working space that enables you to be productive, not get distracted and have a work-rate that supports you producing a publishable book in the shortest possible time is vital. This does not however need to be a dedicated office, though this can help, anywhere you decide is your workspace or workspaces is fine as long as you set it up to meet your needs and you can access it with the minimum of fuss.

The working area should be comfortable, have enough space for you to work on a computer (desktop or laptop), make notes, use reference material (one notebook and one reference book) and have a place for a cup of coffee. How big does this have to be? A small garden table and chair are fine. This can even be a fold up type that you can quickly open out and start working. If you have a desktop computer then you will need to have this set up permanently. Select a spot where you can work unhindered, again this does not necessarily mean a quiet spot, but you do not want to be distracted by the TV. If you have to share the computer with the family then have a booking system!

If you are working in time slots that are no more than an hour at a time and no more than two hours a day then the table and chair set up is less important unless you have a back condition. If you are regularly working longer hours then spend some time setting your monitor height and chair position to reduce the risk of aches and pains.

It is important you keep all of your working documents, notes, and reference material together and easily accessible. Use a basket or box with handles so that you can move it around and easily store it. The box needs to be big enough to hold a notepad, pens and pencils, memory stick, dreams folder (see chapter 4), progress chart and one or two reference books. Keep it where you can access it quickly.

Do I need a computer?
You need access to a computer and the internet; ideally this should be one you can use at a time to suit you so having your own is a benefit. If you don't have a computer then you can still write your book, find out where you can get free or cheap access to a computer with internet access, try your local library or community centre. It might be that your employer is happy for you to use one

at work after hours or during your break. Whilst using a computer away from home may seem a disadvantage at first you will certainly be focussed when you sit down to type those words.

Do I need expensive software?
No. Whilst Microsoft Word is clearly popular, if you don't have it you don't need to buy it. There are several word-processing and office packages available to you free of charge. Consider OpenOffice or LibreOffice, both are free to download, have an excellent range of features and are compatible with Microsoft Word. You also get a spreadsheet and presentation software as well! Think about the features you really need to be able to type your words. Some basic formatting features such as bold and italic, outline features are useful though not essential, as is the facility to create hyperlinks.

The only other software needed is an internet browser; you probably already have this on your computer however these are also freely available.

This chapter contains a list of useful software available free of charge. You may like to look at some of these and decide if they would be of use to you.

What do you really need to get started?
Essentials

Access to a computer
Word-processing software (available free)
Notebook
Pen and pencil
Access to the internet

Desirable

Dictionary
Thesaurus
Graphics software (available free)
Mobile phone (with camera and Apps)

Backing-up your work

Whilst on the topic of computers and software it seems a good idea to raise the important issue of backing-up your work. Be assured that if you do not back-up your work you will lose it.

When someone's computer packs up, no matter how expensive that computer was, they are not interested in whether or not it can be repaired, they want to know if their data can be recovered.

Why does it matter so much? Write your 20,000 words and then delete them permanently; don't actually do this but imagine how you would feel if this happened.

So how do you safeguard your work? Firstly ensure you save as you go along, do not rely on automatic saving features, save every few minutes, if you write that perfect sentence - save it, if you have just completed 100 words – save it.

At the end of each writing session back-up your work to somewhere other than your computer using a memory stick or CD-ROM. If you are using a memory stick then protect it, don't just throw it into a bag or leave on the window sill.

From time to time you need to do a full hard disc back-up to ensure you have all of your photos, movies and music safe.

Finally save to the clouds. There are many online services that give you free space. You can then access your work from anywhere with an internet connection. This method also protects your work in the event of fire or flood. Dropbox is one such service that enables you to automatically save onto your computer and to the clouds as long as you are connected to the internet, you get access anywhere in the world with an internet connection, and, most importantly, it allows you to automatically synchronise your work across more than one computer, netbook and desktop, saving you the hassle of remembering which is the most current version of your work. All you then need to do is the extra back-ups to a memory stick or CD.

Music

Here's another question that frequently gets asked, "Is music a distraction?"

Music can really help you focus, it tends to be non-intrusive whilst at the same time blocking out other distractions. Use a CD player or iPod rather than a radio. If you turn on the radio you will start listening to the presenters and inevitably become engaged with the discussions. Select music that you like and don't play it too loudly. Earphones are fine. When you become focussed on your writing you will find the time goes quickly and before you know it your playlist has finished and you may not even notice the silence.

The mobile office

Anytime, anywhere – having an office you can set up quickly wherever you are can really increase your productivity. There will always be times when you need to be somewhere other than at your desk but are not actively engaged in the action; waiting in the car whilst your children have their sports lesson, sat on a train, even having lunch in a fast food outlet in-between appointments.

All you need to make the most of these times is a small bag containing a netbook, notepad and pens.

Always carry a notepad and pen with you in case ideas, power words or marketing ideas pop into your head. Where practical keep your laptop or netbook with you and always take it when you know you will, or even may, have some writing time available. That way when you are sat in the car park you can fire up and write. Even ten minutes writing time will get 400 words done.

Ensure you keep your netbook running at optimum speeds. Do not install unnecessary software or allow it to run applications in the background. From time to time it can be useful, after backing-up your data, to restore your netbook to its original settings.

The office in your pocket

You can carry everything you need in your pocket and be ready to write whenever you have a few minutes or an idea strikes. A mobile phone with a note taker, voice recorder, camera and internet access will enable you to work on almost any aspect of your book wherever you are.

Use your note taker or voice recorder to write the next section of your book. Take photos to use on the cover or illustrate your work. Access the internet to undertake your research.

A mobile phone is one of the best tools you can have to help you make your non-writing time (planning, research) as productive as possible and enable you to add extra writing slots when the opportunity arises. Any mobile that comes with, or allows you to install, a collection of useful Apps will help increase your productivity by ensuring you do not lose any of those ideas, great opening sentences or thoughts for your next chapter.

Whilst out walking the dog you can start your next writing session; you already know the topic you are going to cover and have completed your initial research so just switch on your voice recorder and start dictating the next paragraph. Save this and type it up during your next writing session or use speech to text software to do the work for you.

If you are not comfortable talking into your phone in public then use the note taker to write your next section, no-one notices if you are "texting" whilst walking. You can email this to yourself and copy into your book.

See something that either sparks an idea or would be a useful image to illustrate your book. Use the camera feature, mobile phone cameras now create high quality images, save the image and email it yourself with some notes.

A timer is great for counting down a fifteen minute writing slot. Note your word count at the beginning and end of the session.

Mindmaps can be used to help generate ideas or plan your book. There are paid for and free Apps available.

Calculator – use this to work out how many books you need to sell this month to generate your target income.

Could you write your entire book on a phone? Yes, use every available five minutes and you will soon have that first draft finished.

Ten free tools to get your writing done
Word-processing/office software – the two to mention here are:
OpenOffice - http://www.openoffice.org/, and LibreOffice - http://www.libreoffice.org/. Both offer a suite of office programmes including a word-processor, spreadsheet, presentation software and more.

Voice to text – Dragon Dictation is a free App that enables you to dictate your text using your mobile phone and then email it, usually to yourself, enabling you to copy this directly into your book.

Mind-mapping – Edraw is a freeware product, a paid for version is available, that can be used when generating ideas and planning your book.

Convert for Kindle – Mobipocket Creator - http://www.mobipocket.com/ - to convert books prior to uploading to Kindle. It is not essential but enables you to preview your books on a Kindle or Kindle App and see any formatting errors.

Online storage – Dropbox – https://www.dropbox.com/ - not only offers you free online storage space but provides you with the tools to synchronise your work across more than one computer. If you work on a laptop and desktop computer, save your work into your Dropbox folder and your work will be saved to your hard drive, online, and also synchronise to your other computers.

Graphics software – Gimp – http://www.gimp.org/ - provides you with all the tools you need to create and edit images and photos; great for creating book covers or illustrating your work.

Dictionary – Cambridge Dictionaries Online – http://dictionary.cambridge.org/ - this is one of many excellent dictionaries available to you online.

Encyclopaedia - http://www.encyclopedia.com/ - again this is one of many. A word of caution with all online resources, check your facts as some online resources may include errors (often typing errors), a good resource will include the source so often you can check this.

Learn to touch type -
http://www.bbc.co.uk/schools/typing/ - aimed at kids but this is an excellent resource that will have your typing speed up in no time.

Writing prompts generator – If you need to kick-start the ideas generation process or want to practise with a writing exercise then Write Sparks - http://writesparks.com/ - will provide you with enough prompts, first lines and words to get you started every day for quite some time. There are paid for versions also available.

4 - Motivation and momentum

As you start writing your 20,000 words there will be times when you feel that you will never reach the end, you will doubt you are good enough and you will still find, despite your greatest efforts, that time thieves take away some of your writing time. It is important you stay motivated and keep going, do this and you will complete your book.

To help keep focussed you are going to complete two small tasks. The first is to remind yourself why you are writing; the second is to recognise the progress you are making.

Purchase a ring binder or similar folder into which you can insert pages. Put a few poly pockets into this to make the next part easier.

Collect images that reflect your dreams, maybe an image of a writer working in their garden room, perhaps a beach on a tropical island, maybe a family picnic, what about that Mercedes you've been dreaming about; whatever it is that inspires you to write.

Place these images into your file, inside the poly pockets if that is easier. When you have doubts or start wondering why you are getting up before the sun rises you can pick up this file and remind yourself what you are aiming for. Over time add more images and notes, you may even remove images as your dreams become more focussed or as you start to realise your dreams will become reality. This file is your dreams folder.

You also need to create a progress chart to ensure you recognise how far you have come, you can maintain this on a computer but I also recommend having this as a paper based chart so you can instantly see how close you are to completing your book.

You could create a simple list like the one below and cross off the tasks or word count as you go. If you prefer you might like to create a table or line graph to plot your word count. Whichever method you use make sure you keep it up to date and look at it regularly so you can see how much you have achieved.

Progress towards completed book
~~Generating an idea~~
~~Research~~
Writing
 - 500 words

- 1000 words
- 1500 words
- 2000 words
- etc

Editing - words
Editing - spelling
Editing - formatting
Title
Cover

5 - Six habits of every successful writer

You are almost ready to start. Develop the habits below and you will become a productive and successful writer.

1 - Record it
Every book you ever read about writing will tell you to carry a notebook and pen everywhere. Good advice, even better though is to start using the voice recorder on your mobile phone. You can speak considerably faster than you can write or type and you won't lose your flow. Dragon Dictation is available as a free App, you can say what you're thinking, the App turns this into text, and then you email it to yourself. The text can then be copied into your book or ideas file. As soon as an idea comes to you - an idea for a book, a title, an inspiring sentence or a new way to sell more books - get out your notebook or phone and record it. If you see it, hear it, read it, or think it, make sure you record it.

2 - Schedule it
If you want to finish your book and start selling copies you need to schedule in the time. Not just a vague "one hour today to do some writing" but:

Morning – 6.30–7.00 write section on "The first post boxes in Britain" – 1200 words
Evening - 5.30–5.45 write section on "Introduction of the postage stamp" – 1200 words
Night – 10.30–11.00 think through content for section on "post box shapes".

Now that you have planned to write each of these sections and have already completed your preliminary research, you should be able to type, or dictate, and complete the 1200 words, half or your daily writing target, at each session.

Of course you will have noted that there is a night-time "thinking" slot; this is because it can be useful to make a start on a section before you go to bed. Unless you really are a night owl then often these late slots are not a good time to write fast, thinking about the section however enables you to start the planning process ready for the next day. When you get up for your 6.30am writing slot you will know exactly what you are going to write and can get the words down fast.

3 - Plan it

The most important part to getting your book completed fast is detailed planning. Get this right and your book will almost write itself. You still have to get the words down but if you have a detailed outline you will be able to fill in the blanks a section at a time, when you sit down to write you will already have the words in your head, you just type away. The more detailed your outline the faster you will write. Spend the time developing this and you will recoup that time back tenfold. How many times have you stared at a blank screen wondering what to write, what comes next, is it relevant. From now on plan your book then sit down and write it – fast. See chapter 8 – Creating an outline.

4 - Set daily writing goals

If you create a plan and schedule your writing you will already have your goals however make sure they are explicit and make sure they are daily goals. If you set the vague goal of 12,000 words by the end of the week you will be almost guaranteed that by Friday you will have achieved very little. Monday you may make a start but you won't hit your 2,400 words a day average. Tuesday someone will ask you out for a drink – you think fine because you can catch up on Wednesday and so it goes on. Set daily goals and achieve them. If you find that 2,400 words a day is still too vague split this into morning, lunchtime, evening goals (which of course will match your schedule). Write your goals down and tick them off.

5 - Track your progress

You have been writing for the last hour and feel that the nine words you have produced is very little progress towards your ultimate goal. The reality is that you are now a step further to completing your book. Set your goals, schedule the activity needed to achieve them and then plot your progress. It is important you recognise that the hour it took to generate a two word title with a seven word sub-title has moved you closer to publishing your book.

6 - Write every day

Another tip you will read in every writing book. Put simply the more you write the faster your book grows. However not all of your writing will be towards the completion of your book; when you have published your book you will also write stunning descriptions of your book, engaging blogs that will encourage people to buy your book, "call to action" emails that will drive readers to make that purchase and of course the outline for your next book. All of this will ensure you stay tuned to new opportunities, improve your words and also speed up the writing process.

6 - Generating ideas
Hour 1

Here are five ways guaranteed to help you generate ideas. Use them and you will never be short of an idea – ever. Each time you decide to write a book, article or blog post you will have a whole list of topics to choose from. Some you may discard because they do not interest you but most you will be able to use today. They may even be large enough to inspire a series!

First you need to decide whether to write a fiction or non-fiction book. Now if you have an idea for a novel that is bursting to get out then by all means write it, this method for writing a book in 30 hours works for both fiction and non-fiction. However consider that non-fiction is usually sold at a higher price and therefore you will achieve a higher income from each copy sold, also readers often buy a number of books on a non-fiction subject so you may be able to tap into a ready-made market, and, currently, non-fiction still outsells fiction.

Try each of the idea generators below and come up with a list of books you could write.

Magazines – visit your local newsagent or supermarket and look at the covers of the various magazines for men and women. What articles are promoted on the front cover? You might find - 10 ways to de-clutter your home, feed a family for a week for just £20, make money from your junk, get fit during your lunch break. The fact these topics have been promoted on the cover suggests that there is a market for this information.

Non-fiction – select one of these topics and expand on it. Or combine more than one. For example you could write a book that takes a room by room approach to de-cluttering a home and combine this with making money from unwanted items. You might be able to take the fitness topic and write a whole book on getting fit using short periods of time and accessible resources such as a staircase.

Fiction – using these topics you can put together some themes or what ifs. Consider the de-clutter topic - what if two people meet and go on a date, one is extremely tidy and minimalist whilst the other keeps everything and is untidy. This could be developed as a comedy, the tidy person tries to "help" the untidy person who then can no longer find anything including the car keys, they end up late for work which has its own set of consequences. Or you could develop this idea as a thriller; could someone be driven to murder because household items are not put back in the correct place?

Tourist information office – collect information on local places of interest or places with a common theme. Visit your local town, what can you discover? The little known facts, places to eat, history, well known people who live, or lived, there, and buildings of interest. Pick up leaflets, what do they suggest to you? Local or national, small museums, free places to visit, rainy day places, cycle tracks, local newspapers or magazines, gardens, architecture.

Non-fiction – create a walking history guide that takes in places of interest; your guide could include lots of interesting snippets and photos.

Fiction – could some of this information provide locations for your book? Maybe a ghost story where two people meet whilst visiting a historic location, perhaps joining in with a group and a tour guide, could they both be from the past – but different centuries. You could develop this as a romantic comedy as they point out inaccuracies and disagree on some of the information given by the tour guide.

Morning TV programs – turn on the TV first thing in the morning (the only time to watch TV as part of your work) and listen to the magazine style programmes. What are the hot topics? Some of these topics could be important right now, write your book in a week and you really could corner the market.

Hobbies – holidays, history, music, sport, food, if you are interested then others will be too. Share your knowledge and experiences. Use your local knowledge, gather hints and tips, what about those "off the beaten track" places that are worth visiting.

Existing books – have you ever said, "I wish I'd written that," well write it! You already know you should never plagiarise work but you can reuse ideas, in fact many classic stories have been retold over and over again. How many times have you read, or watched a film, about two people in love having to face the challenges of the rivalry between their families, often with tragic consequences – think Romeo and Juliet.

As we have already mentioned people often buy several non-fiction books on the same topic; many books will use the same sources of information so select a popular book and make a note of the bibliography. How many fiction and non-fiction books have been written, and sold, about the Titanic?

Non-fiction – select a topic and pick up two or three books from your local library. Note down the chapter names, topics covered and any other relevant information. Use the general topics as the basis for your book or select one chapter that has the potential to be expanded. If you selected a general gardening book you could develop the chapter on gardening in small spaces.

Fiction – take a well-known story or a book you particularly enjoyed. Note down the theme. Consider the different aspects of the book and change them; dates, location, gender, names, jobs, culture, family background, motivation. Take the family rivalry theme – you could have a couple who are committed to each other, all is going well however their parents have different values. There are plans to build a new road through a nature reserve, one set of parents choose to protest against the road whilst the other runs a business that is at risk of going under if the road is not built. Where do the couple's loyalties lie? What pressure will the parents put on them? Could this lead to tragedy?

You now have an extensive list of possible topics. Next you need to select one topic that interests you and you have some basic knowledge of; this will become your book.

Make a list of ideas for your book, look at these and select the three that interest you the most.

Look at each of these and consider how much you already know about the subject.

Make a list of the benefits of the book to a potential reader. Keep these notes as they will be useful when promoting your book.

Select the one idea that you believe will hold your interest for the next 29 hours and beyond as you write, publish and sell your book.

10 ideas you can use to get you started

Don't worry if you think everyone will be using these ideas; these ideas are vague and even is someone else takes the same angle as you it will still be your book. All of these ideas will start you thinking about other angles and perhaps even a series. All could form the basis of a fiction or non-fiction book.

 - Footpaths in your area

- Oldest churches in Britain
- Historic biography(s) – the 8 wives of Henry 8th
- Breakfast to aid success in the classroom
- Inland beaches
- History of wool
- Engaging young people in politics
- Active at 80 – exercises for body and mind
- Set up an online shop
- Decorate on a shoestring

At this stage you have decided on the topic for your book and are now ready to undertake the initial research.

7 - Research - part one
Hour 2

Just enough is enough

You have your idea and now you need to undertake just enough research to enable you to complete the majority of your book. Later on you may need to spend a short time filling in gaps and checking facts but during this hour you will get the majority of your research done.

Stay focussed – you are going to use the internet and you must not get drawn into distractions; no emails, no reading the news, no checking Facebook.

Have a pen and paper handy and also open a text document to copy web addresses and other sources of information. Open Google or your preferred search engine. Type in the subject of your book or a word related to it, ignore the sponsored links, click on the first site and skim read. If there is anything relevant copy the web address into your text document, make some brief notes and highlight keywords relating to the content; these words may later become chapters or sub-headings. You might want to give the site a star rating.

Select another site – repeat as above.

Look at your list of sources and notes, can you refine your search based on some of the key words you have highlighted. Again copy the web addresses and make some brief notes.

By the end of the hour you should have enough material to create your structure and start writing your book.

Plagiarism

A word about copying and plagiarism; never do it. There is no copyright on ideas however if you copy a section of someone else's work you set yourself up for trouble – court case, fines, loss of reputation. If you read something of interest ensure you rewrite it in your own words. Beware of websites that say "free to use", you need to spend time checking if they are legitimate. Read the source information, make some brief notes, and then rewrite.

8 - Creating an outline
Hours 3 – 4

Quick and easy ways to plan your whole book

Creating a structure or outline for your book is key to successfully completing your writing fast. Spend the time getting this as detailed as you can and you will be able to complete your book in 30 hours.

Why is the outline so important? If you have an outline you will always know exactly what you need to write. You will never be sat looking at a blank screen wondering what to type next; you will know. You will not have to start at page one and keep going until you type "the end." You will be able to complete any section at anytime. You will be able to type, or dictate, fast and without hesitation, the words will flow. You will be highly effective during your writing time and you will achieve your word count.

If you want to complete a publishable book in the fastest possible time then read through this chapter and follow the steps precisely. You have a choice about which approach to take when creating an outline however the end result is the same – a detailed outline of your book. As a bonus you will also have 500 words completed.

Creating an outline involves breaking down your 20,000 words into small chunks. If you are writing non-fiction you will create ten chapters and an introduction, you will then further divide the chapters into five sub-sections with approximately 400 words per section or a 10 minute writing session; if you are writing fiction divide you book into 50 scenes, you can create the chapters later, at this stage each scene is an average 400 words, again a 10 minute writing session. Note that for fiction you may choose to create a mix of long and short scenes, you can do this as you build your outline.

Read through the outlining methods below and select the one that works for you.

Index cards - purchase a set of index cards, if possible select those that come in a box and already allow you to sub-divide using letters or, preferably, numbers.

Take one card – write your working title on here, do not spend any time on this as you are going to create a title later. This goes at the front of your box.

Non-fiction - Take 12-14 cards, these are going to be your chapters. On each one write a chapter heading, again these are only working titles and can be just a subject or topic. Have a look at these, rate them based on relevance and available information. Keep only your top ten. Do not discard the others cards just yet as you may want to include these topics somewhere in your book.

For each of your chapters you need 6 index cards for your sub-headings. On each card write a word, statement or question related to your chapter. This time select the strongest 5. Do this for each chapter.

On each subheading card write a few words, a question, piece of information, website address, anything that gives you the basis for your paragraphs. If you find you have too many statements you may need additional sub-headings or chapters – or maybe a second book!

Finally look at the discarded cards, do you need to include anything from these, are they subheadings or paragraphs. If yes add them where they best fit or compile a final chapter of further information.

Place all of your cards into the box using the dividers to indicate the different chapters.

Fiction – take 50 cards. On each card write a brief summary of the scene. Include the purpose of the scene, location and characters involved.

For example – purpose is to show that Sally (main character) is torn between supporting her partner and her father. Whatever she decides will upset one of them possibly meaning they will leave her life for good. In local cafe with best friend for a chat. During lunch break so short of time. Needs to make a decision today.

At this stage you may not know where in the book this scene will fit. What you do need to do however is ask questions that need to be answered either before, during or after this scene, e.g. why does Sally need to make a decision today? Pop these questions in your notebook and cross them off as you answer them. If you have a scene where Sally's father has a heart attack you may want to make reference to a heart condition earlier in the book, don't worry about it yet just make a note in your notebook.

Complete further scenes deciding if the scene comes before or after the ones you have created. If I describe a scene where Sally goes to see her father to let him know what she has decided then this would come after the cafe scene. I might also describe a scene where she sees her partner to let him know her decision; this is after the cafe scene but is it before or after seeing her father?

If you decide that a scene will be longer than 400 words then write x2 or x3 at the top of your card and remove the appropriate number of blank cards from your pile.

Go back through your notebook and add in anything that needs to be added in an appropriate place.

Put your cards in scene order and place in the box. You may want to work out approximate chapter lengths at this stage however, for fiction, you can do this after you have completed all of the scenes.

There you have it, your outline in a box.

Mind mapping

This is great if you like to work visually. You can either use a large sheet of paper or a mind-mapping tool on your computer or mobile phone.

Use a mind-map to explore topics, characters, scenes, locations or anything else related to your book.

Use colour and shapes to indicate different aspects of your book.

If you complete this task on paper you may like to photograph your work so you have a record available on your computer or phone should you need to refer to your mind-map when you are away from your desk.

Outlining using a word-processor

Whichever method you use to outline your book you will ultimately transfer this to your word-processor; you may prefer to create your outline directly onto the computer.

Open a new document in the word processor of your choice and select the outlining tool.

Type your working title; format this as a level 1 heading.

Non-fiction - type in 12 or so chapter titles, these should all be formatted as level 2 headings.

Under each of the level 2 headings type the questions, statements, sources etc. That will form your 400 word sub-sections. Format these as level 3 headings.

Under each level 3 heading type anything relevant, perhaps a source of information or "include quote from doctor here." Format these as body text.

The benefit of using this feature is that you can collapse your structure and only see the chapters or sub-headings.

You can also easily move around sections of your book, e.g. you might decide chapter 4 would work better as chapter 6.

Below are outline examples of two books, the first is where each chapter will have the same sub-headings, the second where each chapter will have different sub-headings but has the potential to be a series. Why are we taking this approach? Because you can re-use the outline and reduce your total production time.

At this stage you do not need to worry about the order of the chapters; get it as good as you can; you can always move things around during editing.

The first book is about Kings and Queens of England. Using the initial idea generation, research and planning sessions it followed the book should be divided into Houses and then the names of the Kings and Queens. Again using the initial research it seems logical that the same information should be available for each King or Queen. From this you could produce the sub-headings.

Example 1
Kings and Queens of England
House of ...
King name...
Key dates – born, died and ruled
History outline
Family
Where lived
Battles
Fashion at the time, clothes, hair styles, diet
Key facts
How died

Using 400 words per subsection and discounting the key dates section as this will be a small word count. You will have 2800 words per chapter. Seven rulers and you have hit your word count.

You now have some decisions to make. Less words per ruler, longer book, a series of books.

Example 2
Tourist guide to a town
Town name
Introduction/Brief history
Key historic facts – linked to later chapters – timeline
How to get there
Map
Buildings to visit
Building name
 - Outline history
 - How to get there
 - Opening times if applicable
 - Costs if applicable
 - Accessibility
 - Uses - now and in the past
 - Famous people who lived there
Gardens to visit
 - Sub sections as for buildings
Walks
Key people from history
Places to eat
Parking
Events/festivals
Shopping
Places for kids

This outline requires more detail however you can start to see how this could be used for other towns and cities.

Outlining works for both fiction and non-fiction books. For fiction replace the headings with scene outlines e.g. *John wakes up to the sound of the alarm, he hates the radio because he does not like hearing the news (why? answer in another scene) so has selected the buzzer. He hits snooze as usual – yawning, big bed, alone (further questions to be answered). Wakes up 30 minutes later, dark, looks at expensive watch. There has been a power cut. Late for appointment, show he is angry. Miss train, show running to platform, someone gets in his way. Has to call a taxi, frustrated when told it will be 15 minutes.*

You should now fully appreciate the importance of producing a detailed outline before writing your book if you want to complete in just 30 hours. Spend the time getting this right and you will be able to work on small sections of your book during the time slots you create. Complete your outline and you are ready to start writing.

9 - Writing
Hours 5 – 13

The key to writing fast is to know exactly what you are going to write before you sit down and start typing. Before you start your first writing session and at the end of each session decide what you are going to be writing next; which sub-section and which paragraph. Leading up to your writing time think about what you want to include, if you are on the internet have a look at some key sites, type some questions into Google, record what you find out. Wander around your chosen town, take some photos, ask people questions.

When you sit down to write the words will be there. Don't worry about spelling, typing errors, punctuation or even if you are unsure of a fact. Use some key words, highlight your text or use question marks to remind you to check when you edit or undertake part two of your research; wherever you see **???** you know you need to check these facts. If you discover, or remember, the answer later on you can always schedule in some mini edit sessions but do not stop and research whilst you are writing. You want those 20,000 words written and written fast.

How to write fast
Just say it - speech to text
Let's start with what is probably the fastest way to write your book. No matter how fast you can type – you can speak faster. Many word-processing applications now come with speech to text built in however you can use a dedicated piece of software such as Dragon Naturally Speaking which works with word-processors. Simply dictate your book and watch it appear on your screen. You can supplement this by using a speech to text App for your mobile phone. When you are out walking, sat in a cafe, or in fact anywhere away from your computer you can still write; just dictate into your phone and then copy this text into your book.

Do not edit
Just type, or dictate. You have read this before but it is vital. If you try and edit you will lose the flow and slow down your progress. All the words you need for the paragraph you are writing should be in your head or notes. At this stage do not worry about spelling, typing errors, the most appropriate word, or grammar. Or anything else that means you are going to stop and think. If you are worried you might forget an area you need to check then just highlight it as soon as you have

finished your session or make a note in your notebook. You will not be coming back to this until you have finished your first draft.

Learn to touch type

Invest some of your time learning to type fast. There are many options available including online resources, CDs, or join a class. If you really are thinking of writing for a significant part of your time then this is a worthwhile investment. You could double your speed and improve your accuracy.

Plan your writing session

If you have one hour to write then divide this into 10 or 15 minute sessions. In your diary list what sections you are going to write in each session. Write it, cross it off, move to the next.

Write your book in chunks

Take one heading at a time and complete. You will be able to complete because you have done your research and know exactly what you are going to write. When finished start the next chunk.

Get in the flow
Totally focus on the task, do not allow any other distractions into your head. If some issue keeps popping up then write it in your notebook so you can attend to it later. Only one exception – if you smell smoke....

Remove distractions
Turn off your email, no pop-ups to say you've got mail. Do not use the formatting features in your word-processor (this is editing), use full screen, turn off the radio and TV, and turn off the phone.

Set a timer
When it comes to focus this is the number one tool. You need to type as much as you can before your time runs out, as the seconds tick by you will find yourself typing faster and faster.

Write during your optimum times
Everyone has their best time of day to write. You don't always get to use this time but at least know when this is so that, when the opportunity arises, you can make best use of it. Many people schedule their editing sessions during the morning as they find they pay more attention to detail. During the evening some people are more creative so use this time to generate new ideas

and think up killer phrases for their marketing material. Write when you can; however, if you have the opportunity to plan tasks at times that enable you to be more productive then you will complete your book at a faster rate.

Plan your book

Many writers think and type; even with reasonable preparation you will find you are typing at around 11 words a minute which is an average "thinking and writing" speed. This is absolutely fine if you want to work on your book for the next year but, by investing a bit of time into the planning (chapter 8), you could easily reach 40 words a minute. If you know what you are going to write you can quickly reach 30 or 40 words a minute even if you have not learned to touch type. Dictate your words and you will reach speeds of over 100 words a minute.

10 - Research - part two
Hour 14

At this stage you will have completed the first draft of your book and be looking at 20,000 words; quite an achievement. Along the way you will have been making notes about anything you need to check, this might be facts or to gather some further information on a topic. These notes will either be in your notebook or highlighted in your text. Either way work through them one at a time, find the information you need and write it into your book.

If you are checking facts aim to use more than one source to ensure your information is accurate.

If it is general information or ideas make some brief notes first to ensure you write everything in your own words.

Go through your notes one at a time and cross off the items as you go.

Your book is now ready for editing.

11 - Editing
Hours 15 – 25

Engage, enthuse and inspire – as a writer this is what you aim to do, get this right and your readers will not only stay with you but they will come back for more. They will want each and every one of your books; they will recommend your work to their friends and, as real fans, will support you on your journey to success.

For any book you need to allow at least as long for the editing stage as for the writing stage. You will make three passes of your work, each with a different purpose. This helps you focus only on what you should be doing and therefore speed the whole process up. Do not be tempted at this stage to do a major rewrite or add additional information. If you do you will take considerably longer to complete your book as you may need to go back and look at your structure. If you have ideas as you go through makes notes in your notebook and then either use them to write a second book or, at a much later date, use them to update your original book and publish as a new edition.

There are at least three stages to editing; the first is to ensure you are writing using words and phrases that hook your readers. You want your readers to invest their time in you, to trust you, to believe in your knowledge and, ultimately, because you have made a positive difference to their lives, purchase future titles. Do this and you will watch your sales rise.

The second is to check and correct any typing, spelling or grammatical errors. Mistakes say one thing to your readers "I am an amateur." If you want to be considered a professional then your book needs to be error free. One sure fire way to turn off your readers is to introduce spelling errors or include a misplaced apostrophe.

The third is to ensure consistency of formatting and remove any formatting that may not be displayed when your book is converted for publication. If you publish for ereaders the reader can choose the font size and other formatting features so any work you do to make your book look professional will be lost; keep it simple.

Power words and emotion
To ensure your readers keep coming back for more you need to write sentences and use words

that speak to the reader; words that draw on their emotions, dreams and fears.

Work on one paragraph at a time, read it aloud, does it flow, does it send the right message. If not – rewrite it.

Look at each word; does the word add the right amount of emotion and intensity? Will your reader feel that this book relates to and is relevant to them?

Here are some examples of words that mean almost the same thing but give very different messages:
Erased/eradicated/obliterated
Big/vast
Flawless/perfect/excellent
Hard/difficult/challenging.

Note that the words have "almost" the same meaning, change the word and you may change the message so read aloud again. You may find it useful to have a thesaurus and dictionary to hand. Whether fiction or non-fiction your aim is to add passion to your writing; if you believe in what you are saying then so will your readers.

Tell a story, even in non-fiction, if you write a guide to a local town you might write something like this "standing in the narrow alleyway I could almost feel the vibration of the soldiers' footsteps as they passed through on their way to such an unpleasant death." Two points here; could you use a more emotional word than unpleasant – painful, predictable, dramatic, untimely, tortuous - and have you done enough to hook the reader to find out how they died?

Spelling and grammar

Most spelling errors are actually typing errors and you just need to correct them. Do be aware of commonly misspelt words and ensure you are using the correct spelling, for example - their, there, they're.

Use a dictionary to check spellings and usage.

It may be useful to print your work and check the paper copy. This can make it easier to see spelling errors that you may have missed on the screen. Highlight errors and then return to the computer to make changes. You will print your work when you have completed your book to undertake a final check.

Formatting – keep it simple
Follow these simple rules:
 - One space after a full stop
 - For emphasis only use bold, underline or italic
 - Do not use tabs
 - Use a soft return if you want an extra line space (if publishing an ebook).

At this stage you have a completed book that is ready for those final elements required before publication.

12 - Completion
Hours 26 – 30

Title

Titles are the first bit of publicity your potential reader will be exposed to; they are also used by search engines on the internet and online book sellers. You need to ensure that the title captures the reader's attention and gives them an idea about what they will get from the book. Your title makes a promise to your reader and your book must deliver that promise. If you have written a novel then a short (or long) title is fine. If you have written a non-fiction book then have a short title with a longer subtitle. This is particularly useful if you are going to publish an ebook.

A good way to start building your title is to think of all the words you might put into a search engine to find information on your subject. If your book is about creating healthy meals for children then you might use children, kids, food, healthy, cooking, fast, recipes, lunchbox, tasty, appealing. You could even put some of these words, or phrases, into Google and see what else comes up. You will probably find other phrases are suggested which will give you even more words to add to your list.

Use your thesaurus to find other words with a similar meaning.

You may come up with the title, "Food for Kids – quick and easy meals to keep your children happy, healthy and wise."

Compare this title to the content in your book, does the book deliver on the promise. It might be well known that eating well can improve learning but does your book refer to this, if not lose the word "wise."

When you have finally decided on your title pop it into Google and see if any other books have the same title. Not necessarily a problem but you might prefer something unique.

Write an introduction

For a non-fiction book you need to write an introduction to go before the main content. The introduction should welcome the reader and invite them in. It should outline the content or purpose of the book and also highlight the benefits of buying and reading the book. If you publish for Kindle the potential reader may download a free sample which will probably include the introduction; you need to ensure the reader wants to make that purchase.

The introduction should highlight the challenges faced by the reader and state how this book will provide solutions. You could include some comparisons to other solutions and highlight why the content in your book is a better option. Tell the reader why you are an expert on this subject.

If you are stuck for ideas then read the introduction to other books and make notes on the different approaches.

When you have written your introduction, edit it. Make these words the best that you can, ensure there are no errors. The introduction is part of your marketing toolbox.

Complete the contents page

You will need to create a contents page for your book. It is important you do this manually and not use the automatic features available with some word-processing software (if publishing an ebook). The contents page will simply be a list of chapters; do not add page numbers at this stage. If you publish for an ereader then page numbers are irrelevant as screen sizes will be different and the reader can select the font size so the page numbering will change. If you print as a hard copy then you need to get your pages set up correctly before adding page numbers.

Front matter

Your front matter should consist of the title, author, copyright, and year of publication. These are the essentials.

Depending on how you decide to publish you may need to include the words "Kindle Edition" or an ISBN.

You may also choose to include acknowledgements, a disclaimer and a dedication.

Study other books in your chosen publishing format to see what they include and decide how much more than the essentials you want to include.

Back matter

Use the opportunity at the end of your book to promote any additional resources related to you (the author) or the book content. You might like to promote other books you have written, your website or blog, and other services you offer.

You could also use this to promote your next book and give a release date; this will certainly focus you to hit that deadline.

Book cover
The first decision here is do you take the DIY route and create one yourself or do you use a professional service. Remember this is your primary selling tool. It needs to look professional and send the right message. Do not lose that sale because of a poor cover. If you have the design skills required then create your own cover. There are many sites available that have royalty free images available or you might choose to take your own photos. If you take the DIY route – keep it simple. If the cover has an amateur look the reader will perceive the content as being written by an amateur.

Professional services can be relatively inexpensive. You could use a local designer or look online for a service that specialises in book covers; they can often produce something within a few days.

The cover should complement the title and content; again this is about making a promise that will be delivered.

Write your description and blurb

You can save a little time here if you have an introduction written as this can form the basis of your blurb and description; you will already have the content summary, features and benefits, and keywords identified.

The blurb is a short description that is usually found on the back of a book. Whilst you may not need this for an ebook, though you could place it in your front matter, you will find it useful for promotional material such as the home page of a website. A blurb is marketing material and used to encourage the reader to take the next step which is often looking at the contents page and reading the introduction or first page.

Your description is also a marketing tool. This will appear on Amazon if you publish for Kindle and you will want to use it on your website, in your blog, in fact anywhere where search engines search! You need to cover features and benefits as well as content but think about search engine strings, consider what potential buyers will input into Google or Amazon when looking for a book on your subject. Use both short and long strings of words. If you have a maximum number of words available to you – use them all.

As with everything you write ensure you edit your work to remove errors and use powerful language that reaches your potential readers.

Final checks

At this final stage print out a copy of your book and take it away from your computer. Carefully go through and check for any errors you may have missed; looking at your work on paper rather than on screen will help you identify those final corrections. On the paper copy note any amendments needed, do this in a coloured pen so they stand out when you come to apply them to your digital copy.

When you have gone through the whole document it is back to the computer to make the corrections crossing them off the paper copy as you go.

If you find it useful you can ask someone else to do this task for you, sometimes when you are too familiar with your work you read what you think you have written rather than what you have actually written.

That's it you have a completed copy of your book ready to publish and sell.

Now it really is time to congratulate yourself.

What next?
Publish it!
You now have your completed book ready to publish. Now is the time to decide how you want to publish your book – printed copy or ebook. You could of course do both.

Certain types of book are better published as a printed book; for example, if you have written a book about local places of interest you may be able to leave copies of your book at the places you have included and agree a commission with the retailer for copies sold.

If you are going to publish printed copies then you need to decide whether to print a batch of books, which you will have to store, or use a print on demand (POD) service, which will mean that individual copies cost more to produce.

Either way there are services available to support you through the process including obtaining an ISBN and even producing a cover. Some of these services include support with marketing, for example making your book available to bookshops.

Producing an ebook and selling online is probably the quickest and easiest way of making your book available to readers. There are a number of options available to you including using Amazon or selling directly from your own website. Ensure you read all of the terms and conditions and compare options to ensure you make the right choice for you.

Sell it!
Your book is now available to buy but how do you attract potential readers? Once you have written and published your book you need to allocate time to marketing.

The key to effective marketing is to ensure the reader has the opportunity to buy your book at the point you promote it to them. Put some time between the promotional activity and the opportunity to buy and your potential reader will not make that purchase. Here are some ideas to get you started.

Start a blog and write regularly. Write about the topic of your book, the challenges of working from home, or indeed anything that is topical, you want to bring readers back to your blog regularly, the more often they come the more likely they are to buy. Make sure you have an easy "buy it" link to your book.

Set up a website – again keep this up-to-date, it can often be useful to promote books on the same topic as your book, people often buy a number of books on their subjects of interest.

Do readings at the library or bookstore, offer to give talks in historic buildings in exchange for the opportunity to promote your book, attend craft or gift fairs, and give talks to a group of potential customers, maybe a group of gardeners or the Women's Institute.

Plan your marketing campaign now.

And finally!
Start planning and writing your next book.

If you would like further hints and tips on developing your career as a writer then follow my blog at:

www.writepublishsell.blogspot.co.uk

Here you will find up to date information on latest trends, advice on writing, ideas for your books, and how technology can help you write, publish and sell your work.

Also by Adam Jackson

Kindle Edition available on Amazon

Publish it!
How to self-publish your book for free using Kindle Direct Publishing (KDP), CreateSpace and Smashwords

Self-publishing offers incredible opportunities for all writers regardless of the genre, subject or word count. You can write and publish short stories, poems, reports, novels; in fact whatever type of book you have written you can make it available to readers who are actively seeking new and exciting fiction and non-fiction books. The traditional gatekeepers of published works can no longer restrict what is available to the reader.

The benefits of self-publishing are so great that this option is now the first choice for many writers. As the writer and publisher you keep control of price, distribution, cover design, promotion and updates.

Using online services you can publish a printed or ebook for free and have it available to readers in as little as 10 minutes.

Follow the step-by-step instructions in this book and you will be able to:

- Select the best publishing option for you and your book.
- Prepare your book for publication.
- Publish your book for free.
- Select your distribution channels.
- Sell on Amazon, iBookstore, WHSmith, Barnes and Noble, and through other retailers.
- Start selling you book in as little as 10 minutes.
- Keep the profits from your book - royalties can be as high as 85%.
- Maximise sales and income using an effective pricing strategy.
- Write a description to ensure readers find your book online.

There is a huge demand for books by previously unpublished writers; tap into this market and develop a following of readers who will come back time after time to purchase and read your latest work.

This is one market where you are not in direct competition with other writers; if readers enjoy books written on a particular subject or in a specific genre they will look for, and buy, more of the same.

Printed in Great Britain
by Amazon